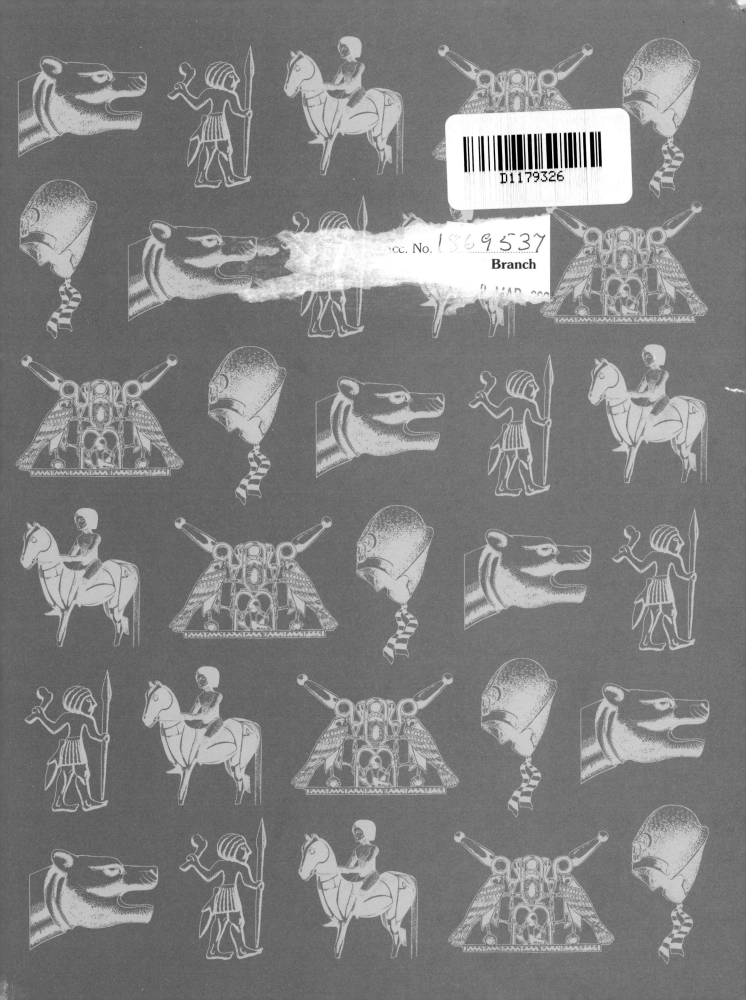

ARMIES OF THE PAST

GOING TO WAR IN
ANCIENT
EGYPT

ARMIES OF THE PAST

GOING TO WAR IN
ANCIENT
EGYPT

Dr Anne Millard

W

FRANKLIN WATTS

LONDON • SYDNEY

ILLUSTRATIONS BY:
Mark Bergin
Giovanni Caselli
Chris Molan
Lee Montgomery
Peter Visscher
Maps by Stefan Chabluk

Editor Penny Clarke
Editor-in-Chief John C. Miles

Designer Steve Prosser
Art Director Jonathan Hair

© 2000 Franklin Watts

First published in 2000
by Franklin Watts
96 Leonard Street
London
EC2A 4XD

Franklin Watts Australia
56 O'Riordan Street
Alexandria
NSW 2015

ISBN 0 7496 3810 9

Dewey classification: 932

A CIP catalogue record
for this book is available
from the British Library.

Printed in Hong Kong, China

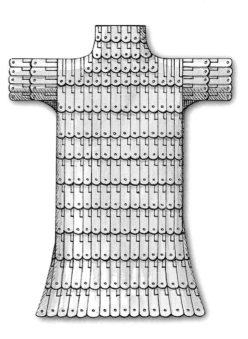

CONTENTS

Predynastic Egypt

By about 5000BC there were many small farming communities in Egypt. Slowly, these communities grew into the two ancient Egyptian kingdoms of Upper (southern) and Lower (northern) Egypt.

These ancient Egyptians had a system of writing, were skilled craftworkers and built mud-brick monuments to their dead kings.

Archaic Egypt

About 3100BC a king of Upper Egypt called Menes conquered the north and united the kingdoms of Upper and Lower Egypt. He built a new capital for the united kingdom at Memphis, although the royal burial-ground was at Abydos.

Early Egyptian gold and amethyst cosmetic jar

THE EGYPTIAN WORLD

Thousands of years ago, the peoples of ancient Egypt lived in an area protected in the north by the Mediterranean Sea and in other directions by deserts and cliffs. They believed that this hard-to-invade land had been given to them by the gods.

Every year the River Nile flooded, bringing water and fertile new soil to the fields beside it. This meant the Egyptians could grow enough food for themselves and even export some. Their land also had gold, copper and good building stone.

These factors made ancient Egypt a wealthy kingdom, but also a tempting target for invaders. To protect their land the Egyptians developed a well-organised and efficient army which enabled the rulers of Egypt to repel attackers and conquer neighbouring peoples for 3,000 years. This helped to preserve the ancient Egyptians' unique culture, so much of which still survives.

Hawks of the god Horus: jewel worn by an Egyptian princess

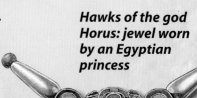

Old Kingdom
c.2700 – 2100BC

This was a period of great achievements in art, literature and science. Kings were buried in huge stone pyramids. Trade flourished.

First Intermediate Period
c.2100 – 2040BC

An unsettled time of civil wars and foreign invasions. A line of kings ruled parts of Egypt from the city of Herakleopolis, but their power was limited.

Middle Kingdom c.2040 – 1790BC

A nomarch (district governor) of Thebes reunited Egypt, beginning a new era of greatness. Neighbouring Nubia was conquered and the army constructed huge fortresses on Egypt's southern and eastern frontiers.

HITTITES

MITTANI

CYPRUS

Orontes

Byblos ● ● Kadesh

MEDITERRANEAN SEA

Megiddo ● CANAAN

Joppa ● ● Jericho

Alexandria ● **LOWER EGYPT**

LIBYA　　Buto ●　● Avaris

Siwa Oasis　**Memphis** ●

Bahriya Oasis　　　*Fayum*　**SINAI**

●
Herakleopolis

Farafra Oasis

UPPER　*Nile*　**RED SEA**
EGYPT

Dakla　　● **Abydos**
Oasis

● **Thebes/Luxor**
Hierankopolis
Kharga Oasis　● **Aswan**

First Cataract

NUBIA

Second Cataract　　Buhen

Semnah

KUSH
Third Cataract

Fourth Cataract

Gebel Barkal ●

The Egyptian Empire

Major forts

Second Intermediate Period
c.1790 – 1550BC
Hyksos invaders from Canaan set up a kingdom in the Nile Delta. Egyptian princes still ruled from Thebes, but had to pay tribute (taxes) to the kings of the Hyksos.

New Kingdom c.1550 – 1080BC
At last the Hyksos were driven out of Egypt, and an era of great wealth and cultural achievement began. Kings were buried in the Valley of the Kings at Thebes.

Kings and Pharaohs
'King' is the term used in this book to describe Egypt's rulers. It is short for 'King of Upper and Lower Egypt'. 'Pharaoh' is not used because it did not become common until the New Kingdom.

Third Intermediate Period
c.1080 – 664BC
A time of weak government and disputed successions, with Libyans, Nubians and Assyrians fighting over the wealthy land. Eventually an Egyptian prince expelled the foreign invaders.

Late Period 664 – 332BC
Another era of territorial and cultural achievements. However, Egyptian kings used Greek soldiers in the Egyptian army, and Greek traders settled in the Delta. Eventually the Persians conquered Egypt.

The lighthouse at Alexandria, c.330BC

Ptolemaic Egypt 332 – 30BC
The Macedonian ruler Alexander the Great drove out the Persians. One of his generals, Ptolemy, became king of Egypt. His descendants ruled until the Romans defeated Queen Cleopatra VII in 31BC and Egypt became part of the Roman Empire.

EGYPT'S FIRST ARMIES

During the Old Kingdom (c.2700 – 2100BC), the kings of Egypt possessed a troop of bodyguards and a small regular army. These forces were usually enough to protect trade and deal with border raids by neighbouring states. All Egyptians owed the king a labour tax, so if more soldiers were required for any reason, taxpayers were called up, trained and sent off to war.

In the Middle Kingdom (c.2040 – 1790BC) Egypt began to build an empire. The kings led large well-trained armies against Nubia. They eventually conquered it and held it as a buffer between Egypt and the warlike peoples of Kush to the south.

Nubian mercenary

MERCENARIES

To increase the size of their armies, many Egyptian kings hired mercenaries (professional soldiers). From around 2000BC onwards, the kings of Egypt paid Nubians to fight for them. The Nubians were renowned for their skills as archers.

EGYPTIAN WARRIOR

Egyptian soldiers of the Old and Middle Kingdoms fought with a variety of weapons and protected themselves with leather-covered wooden shields. For more protection, some soldiers wore leather straps across their chests.

Egyptian warrior of the Middle Kingdom

Wrestling matches helped keep early soldiers fit and agile

 PREDYNASTIC TIMES

Pictures of Egypt's first soldiers show them wielding an assortment of weapons. They have no armour, but wear wild animals' tails, perhaps to show what fierce fighters they are.

 LEADERS

The first Egyptian kings led their troops into battle personally, but by the Old Kingdom kings were considered too holy to fight. In the Middle Kingdom kings became warriors again. The greatest was Senusret III.

 **PRIVATE ARMIES**

Old and Middle Kingdom Egypt was divided into 42 nomes (districts). The nomarchs (district governors) were allowed to maintain private armies for the king to use when he needed. During the unsettled First Intermediate Period (c.2100 – 2040BC), the nomarchs used their armies against each other and even against the king himself.

ENEMIES

BEDOUIN AND CANAANITES

The Bedouin, a nomadic people of the Eastern Desert, often attacked Egyptian trade caravans. Canaanites came from the area of modern Israel. Some traded with Egypt; others, like the warrior above, were hostile.

LIBYANS

To the Libyans of the arid Western Desert (below), Egypt's lush Delta farmland was temptation. Given any opportunity, they invaded. Strong Egyptian kings usually repelled such attacks, but in the First Intermediate Period the Libyans managed to seize land and settle.

NUBIANS AND KUSHITES

Nubians came from the south. They were trading partners and later subjects of the Egyptians. The Kushites lived south of the Nile's Third Cataract and were a great threat to Egypt. They were not conquered until the New Kingdom (c.1550 – 1080BC).

ENEMIES OF EGYPT

The armies of ancient Egypt had to be ready to deal with many rivals, rebels and invaders, such as Canaanites and Syrians, Mitanni, Hittites and Sea Peoples.

In the Second Intermediate Period (c.1790 – 1550BC), Egypt was overrun by the Hyksos, a warlike people from the east. Eventually the princes of Thebes drove the Hyksos out of Egypt.

The Hyksos invasion gave the Egyptians a new spirit of aggression. As as a result they went on to create the greatest empire of its day. Conquering such an empire needed a large, full-time, well-trained army.

Hittite warrior

Syrian archer

Sherden warrior

MITANNI AND HITTITES

Egypt's first great rivals were the Mitanni, from the region now known as Iraq. Then the Hittites (from Anatolia in modern-day Turkey) crushed the Mittannian empire and became Egypt's most dangerous enemies.

SEA PEOPLES

Egypt's northern coasts were raided by the Sea Peoples, including the Sherden and Peleset peoples. Thought to be from Mycenaean Greece, these peoples started raiding Egypt around 1500BC. Some were captured and joined the bodyguard of the Egyptian kings; others remained dangerous enemies.

CANAANITES AND SYRIANS

Egypt conquered most of its eastern neighbours. Some were more powerful than others, but Canaanites and Syrians were both proud and ancient peoples with their own distinct cultures. As a result, they resented Egyptian rule and often rebelled, seeking help from the Mitanni or Hittites, the Egyptians' great enemies.

⚱ CHARIOTS

One reason why the Hyksos conquered Egypt so easily was that they had horses and chariots, both of which were unknown in Egypt. The speed of a chariot made it a devastating weapon which the Egyptians soon learned to use.

The introduction of chariots had a profound effect on Egyptian warfare. Generals had to change their battle tactics to use the chariots to the best advantage and to protect their infantry from the chariots of the enemy.

To make the best use of this new weapon, charioteers and chariot soldiers needed intensive full-time training – and so did the infantry alongside whom they fought in battle. Amateur soldiers were no longer good enough.

'…I let them see your Majesty as a shooting star that scatters fire as it sheds its flame …I let them see your Majesty as falcon-winged, one who grasps what he spies, as he desires.'

The god Amun-Re addresses King Tuthmosis III in his chariot

⚱ FAST AND FURIOUS

Today the world moves very fast, but in ancient Egypt the fastest speed at which you could travel was the speed at which you could run – until the chariot was introduced. In that slow-moving society, the speed of a chariot must have seemed terrifying. But horses and chariots were expensive and

An Egyptian prince drives his chariot and horses at a gallop

quickly became status symbols for the wealthy.

Fighting from one of the Egyptians' light wooden chariots behind a pair of horses driven at full gallop required great skill and strong nerves.

FORTRESSES

The catastrophic invasions and civil wars of the First Intermediate Period (c.2100 – 2040BC) made the Egyptians realise that they needed to guard their frontiers and trade routes effectively.

Around 2000BC the king ordered the building of two lines of fortresses: one along the eastern frontier and the other around the Second Cataract. During the New Kingdom (c.1550 – 1080BC) forts were built on the north-west frontier as a defence against raids by the Libyans and Sea Peoples.

'I have made my boundary further south than my fathers. I have added to what was bequeathed to me. I am a king who speaks and acts – what my heart plans is done by my arm. I am one who attacks to conquer, who is swift to succeed.'

King Senusret III (c.2000BC) praises himself on a boundary stela (stone) set up at Semnah fort

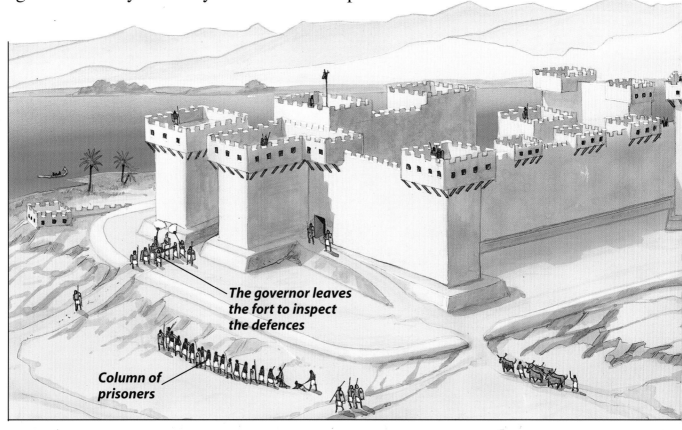

The governor leaves the fort to inspect the defences

Column of prisoners

BUILDING AND DESIGN

Ancient Egyptian forts were immensely strong – the walls of a fort such as the one shown above could be 10 metres high, 5 metres thick and built of nearly 15 million mud bricks.

Many forts had an inner fortified town and an outer enclosure, also heavily fortified. Beyond this lay a deep ditch. Forts in Nubia could be supplied by river and had hidden access to the Nile so that the garrison could draw water. The fort at Buhen had arrow slits that enabled archers to cover every square metre of ground. As examples of military architecture, these forts rival the best medieval castles.

LIFE IN A FORTRESS

Life in an Egyptian fortress was usually busy – the garrison of a great fort such as Buhen probably contained about 2,000 troops and 3,000 civilians. Soldiers patrolled regularly, looking for signs of trouble. Trading caravans had to be guarded and the movements of conquered peoples and anyone crossing Egypt's borders monitored.

The huge fortress at Semnah, near the Second Cataract of the Nile

TRIBUTE

In the ancient world conquered peoples had to pay regular tribute (taxes) to their conquerors in the form of goods, crops or precious items such as gold.

During the New Kingdom Egypt's kings became extremely rich through the taxes paid by their foreign subjects. This detail from a tomb painting (above right) shows a delegation of Syrian tribute-bearers.

Besides tribute, conquered

princes had to send their children to Egypt as hostages. The children were educated at the Egyptian court and treated well, so that when they went home they would be loyal subjects of Egypt.

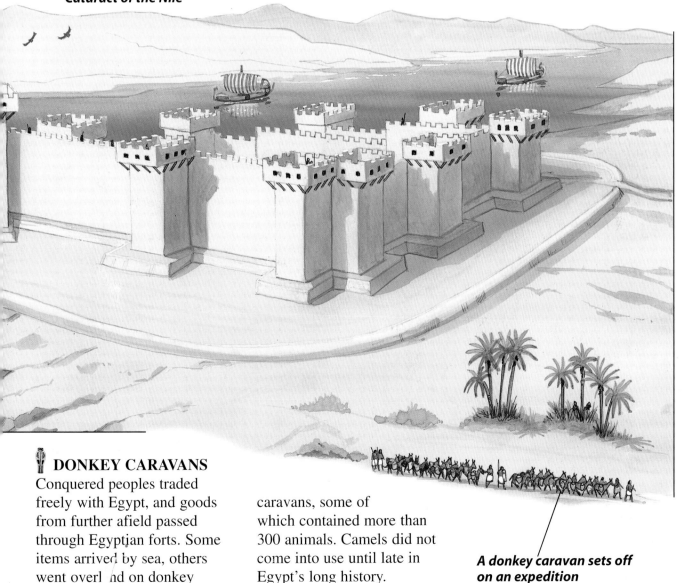

DONKEY CARAVANS

Conquered peoples traded freely with Egypt, and goods from further afield passed through Egyptian forts. Some items arrived by sea, others went overland on donkey caravans, some of which contained more than 300 animals. Camels did not come into use until late in Egypt's long history.

A donkey caravan sets off on an expedition

SIEGE!

If the Egyptians did not defeat an enemy or rebel force in battle, they might besiege one of their forts or walled cities, cutting off supplies of food and water. This was a good way to force the defenders to surrender. Egyptian texts never admit that any of their own cities or forts were attacked and taken in this way, but they do give details of enemy strongholds that were captured.

STARTING A SIEGE

Sculptures and paintings in Egyptian tombs and temples depict only successful sieges. At first, troops surrounded the city to cut off supplies. Then scouts went out to watch for any enemy relief force marching to help the defenders.

LADDERS

Scenes painted in Old Kingdom tombs show Egyptians using ladders to scale the walls of enemy cities. Some of the ladders had wheels so that they could be pushed up to the walls more easily.

Archers on the walls defend the fortress

An Egyptian army lays siege to a fort

TUTHMOSIS III

Tuthmosis III was Egypt's greatest warrior king, winning at least 17 major military campaigns. Laying siege to the Canaanite city of Joppa, he smuggled 200 Egyptian soldiers into the city by hiding them in baskets which were said to contain presents for the enemy queen. Once inside the city walls, the Egyptians climbed out and opened the gates of the city to let in the rest of the Egyptian soldiers.

VICTORY

EXECUTION

After a siege, defeated rebel leaders were executed. The method, as shown above, was to bash their heads in with a mace, although we don't know if the king himself always did it.

CAPTURE

Ordinary prisoners of war became slaves. The king kept some to help build his temples or to work in quarries and mines. Others were given to temples or to soldiers as rewards.

Ramesses II

SELF-PROMOTION

All kings recorded their victories, but never their defeats, because they believed that the gods did not intend Egypt to be beaten. In his account of the battle of Kadesh, Ramesses II managed to turn what was at best a draw into a personal triumph.

BATTERING RAMS

Scenes painted in Egyptian tombs show that troops used battering rams to break down gates and walls. It is clear that there was some sort of covering to protect the soldiers working the device, but there are no details about how the covering was moved forwards.

SLAVES

Prisoners who became household slaves in Egypt were usually well treated, especially if they had a valuable skill, such as carpentry, spinning, weaving or dancing. Egyptian slaves had rights and could even own property.

Nubian slave girl dancing

Reconstruction of a battering ram

'His portion is that on which Re shines ... the southerners come to him bowed down, the northerners on their bellies. He has gathered them all into his fist, his fist has crashed upon their heads, as Amun-Re-Atum has decreed.'

Inscription in praise of King Amenhotep II

TRAINING

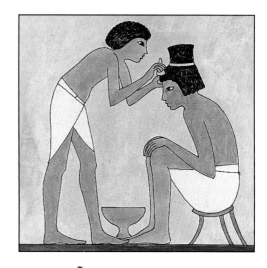

ew Egyptian peasants ever left their villages, so a boy from a small town in Upper Egypt who volunteered for the army would have found the journey down the Nile to Memphis very exciting. The sight of the great city would have been overwhelming, and life in the vast army camp on its outskirts probably rather daunting at first.

Day after day he would have had to march until he was ready to drop. Eventually the raw recruit would have learnt the skills of soldiering and be ready to join an established unit.

☥ HAIRCUT
New recruits to the army got the Egyptian equivalent of a 'short back and sides'.

ARMY MARCHING ORDER

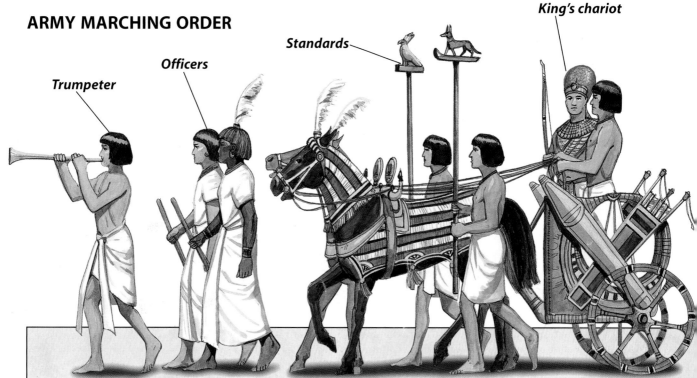

Trumpeter

Officers

Standards

King's chariot

☥ LEARNING THE SIGNALS
During battle, commands such as 'Charge!', 'Retreat!' and 'About face!' were given by trumpet calls, so a new recruit had to learn them all quickly.

☥ ROD OF IRON
Army officers carried staffs and batons. These indicated the officer's rank, but must have also been useful for hitting unruly recruits.

☥ CHARIOTS
A two-horse chariot held a charioteer and a soldier, and each division had 500 chariots. Facing a charge by such chariots was terrifying.

An Egyptian prince learns how to fire a bow

TO BE A LEADER

As well as acquiring weapons skills and learning to drive a chariot, officers also had to study how to plan long-term strategies and tactics. In addition, they learned to coordinate infantry and chariot manoeuvres and studied the geography and customs of the lands in which they would operate.

CONSCRIPTS

Not all soldiers were volunteers. Scribes made lists of able-bodied young men whom the king could call up in turn as part of their labour tax.

'Let me describe to you the woes of a soldier – they are as many as his many officers ... After he has been woken up before dawn, they are after him like a donkey and he works until the sun sets.'

The life of a soldier, from an ancient papyrus

A tomb painting shows the scribe of recruitment besieged by anxious relatives begging him not to take their young men for the army!

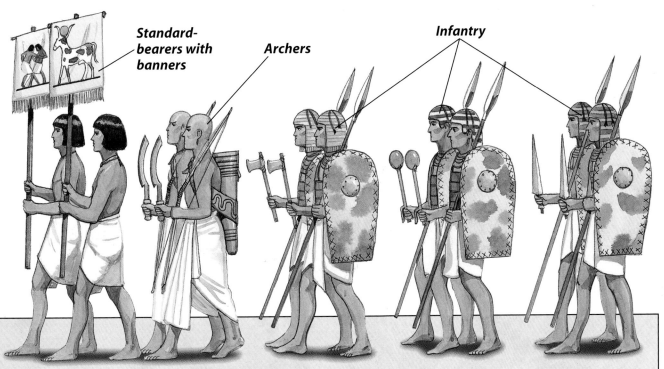

Standard-bearers with banners

Archers

Infantry

RALLYING POINT

The different units of the army all had their own standards. In a battle, the soldiers rallied around their standard-bearer.

CHOOSING A WEAPON

Soldiers were trained to use many weapons, but became experts with one or two only. So each man joined a company that used his chosen weapon.

MERCENARIES

Nubian, Libyan and Sherden mercenaries were common in Egyptian armies until about 1080BC. After that, Greek mercenaries replaced them.

READY FOR BATTLE

Blue war helmet

By the time of the New Kingdom (c.1550 – 1080BC) the army was made up of divisions, each named after a god, such as Amun, Re or Ptah. Each army division contained 5,000 men, of which 4,000 were infantry and 1,000 fought from chariots.

Each division was subdivided into companies of 200 men, led by a standard-bearer, and each had its own title – 'Bull in Nubia', 'Splendour of Aten', and so on. Within each company were groups of 50 men, led by a 'Chief of 50'. Below this, the men were divided into groups of ten, who lived and ate together.

THE BLUE WAR HELMET

New Kingdom kings led their armies into battle in person and wore a distinctive blue war helmet like this. The crown prince was his father's deputy in a battle.

Copper target

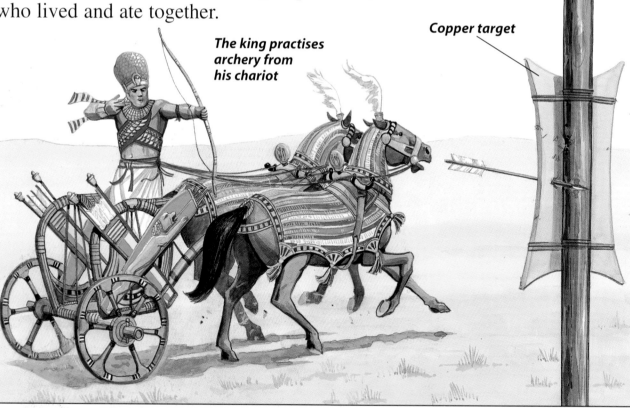

The king practises archery from his chariot

SHOCK TACTICS

The Egyptian army used chariots as mobile fighting platforms, not for transport. Egyptian chariots were light, speedy and easy to manoeuvre. They were used in charges to break up lines of enemy infantry and to help their own when attacked by the enemy.

All the charioteers, chariot soldiers and horses received the intensive training they needed from stable masters at army training stables.

IN THE ARMY

COUNTING HANDS
Scribes kept the army well organised. For example after a battle soldiers cut the right hands off the bodies of enemy dead and put them in piles. Scribes counted up the hands and wrote the number down for the official records.

Wooden carving of a scout

SCOUTS
To assess the enemy's strengths and weaknesses, the Egyptian army used fast-moving scouts mounted on horseback. Horses were not ridden into battle because saddles and stirrups had not been invented and a rider could easily be unseated in a charge.

DAILY PRACTICE
Besides marching and drilling, a recruit had to learn how to handle all types of weapons and had to keep practising every day.

ARMY RANKS
The Egyptian army had a clear ranking system. The king was the commander-in-chief. A general commanded each division, with officers commanding the companies and smaller units. The chariots had their own commander and officers.

Also attached to the army were doctors, priests, scribes, armourers, messengers, heralds, spies, grooms and servants to look after all the soldiers' needs.

ADVISERS AND SPIES
The king had an army council of advisers. He also had someone called the Master of the Secrets of the King working for him. This suggests an organised spy system collecting information for the king.

King

General

Officer

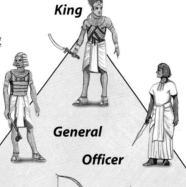

Light skirmisher *Mercenary* *Infantry* *Chariot*

Servant *Cook* *Priest* *Scribe* *Groom and armourers* *Doctors*

WEAPONS AND ARMOUR

New Kingdom infantry contained three kinds of soldiers. The elite troops were the 'Braves' – the commandos of the day. Few in number, they undertook the most dangerous assignments. The bulk of the army were the 'Veterans', seasoned troops who formed the front ranks in battle. Then there were the 'Recruits', less-experienced troops who formed the second ranks and reserves. The Recruits contained both volunteers and conscripts, but most conscripts undertook less dangerous assignments.

PROTECTION

New Kingdom infantry still used shields, but also had thick padded linen helmets and cuirasses (body armour), sometimes reinforced with leather bands or scales. This extra protection was needed because they now had to withstand chariot charges, the new, powerful composite bow and tougher edged weapons made of bronze.

'He is called up for Syria. He may not rest – his marches are uphill through the mountains. He drinks water every third day – it is smelly and tastes of salt. His body is ravaged by illness.'

A teacher tries to persuade his pupil not to become a soldier

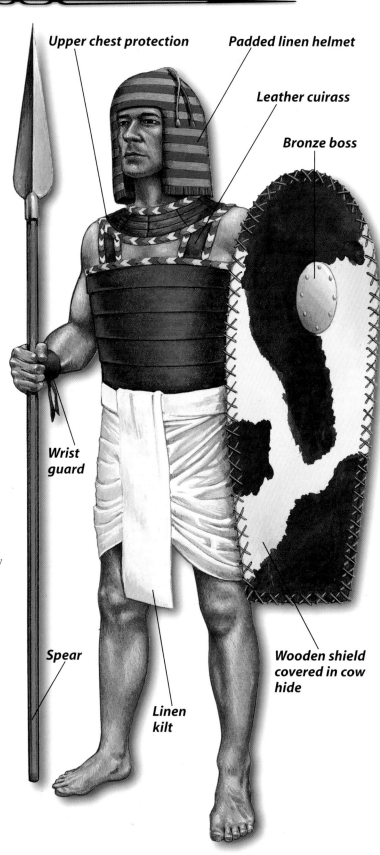

Upper chest protection

Padded linen helmet

Leather cuirass

Bronze boss

Wrist guard

Spear

Wooden shield covered in cow hide

Linen kilt

WEAPONS

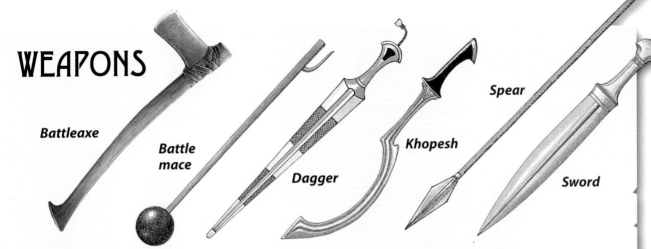

Battleaxe

Battle mace

Dagger

Khopesh

Spear

Sword

BRONZE

While early weapons were made of stone and copper, New Kingdom ones were made of bronze. These are some of the weapons used by Egyptian soldiers. In addition they had javelins for thrusting and bows and arrows.

IRON

By 1000BC some people in the Middle East had discovered the secret of smelting iron. This put Egypt at a disadvantage because it had to import iron to make weapons of comparable quality.

NEW WEAPONS

Besides the horse and chariot, the Hyksos introduced two other weapons, both quickly adopted by the Egyptians. One was the curved sword, the khopesh, and the other was the composite bow. This was stronger than Egyptian bows, so it shot arrows further.

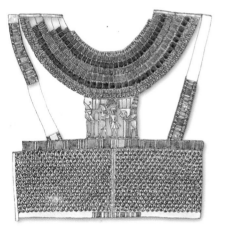

Tutankhamun's ceremonial armour

📖 TOO GOOD FOR BATTLE!

Ceremonial armour made of gold scales inlaid with semiprecious stones was found in the tomb of King Tutankhamun. Also in the tomb was a more practical everyday cuirass made of thick leather scales attached to a linen base. In some paintings kings are shown wearing ceremonial armour shaped like a falcon's wings.

📖 ARCHERS

Archers wore a special brace to protect their wrists from the snap of the bowstrings. Everyday versions were made of leather but the rich used more expensive materials, such a carved ivory version found at Amarna.

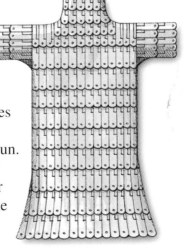

Mail shirt, c.1200BC

Bronze links from a mail shirt

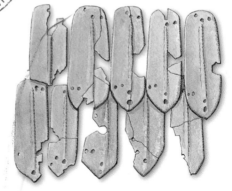

📖 MAIL SHIRTS

Some warriors owned armour made of bronze scales sewn onto a padded linen shirt. This arrangement made the mail shirt flexible, so allowing the wearer to move freely. It was clearly a much better defence against enemy weapons – especially arrows – than leather and linen, but it would have been very expensive and perhaps only used by officers and royalty.

Making camp

When they were on campaign, Egyptian soldiers made camp every night. Workers piled up a mound of earth and planted shields on top to form a defensive wall. This protected the troops within from all but the most determined attack. Behind the wall, troops erected tents in neat rows with the king's tent at the centre and the tent housing statues of the gods close by. Areas were set aside for both the horses and chariots and the donkeys that carried all the supplies.

CAMP LIFE

Servants and doctors looked after the troops, grooms and vets tended the animals, and armourers repaired damaged weapons. There were also priests with the army to look for omens that revealed the gods' will, especially that of Amen-Re, King of the Gods, who personally advised the king when to go to war.

Scouts

Chariots

TENTS

Tents were made of leather, stretched over wooden frames. Ordinary soldiers slept ten to a tent, but paintings of officers' tents (below) show that they enjoyed more room.

SCOUTS

Mounted scouts continually patrolled the area around the camp on fast horses to locate the enemy and make sure that the Egyptian army was not in danger of a surprise attack. Spies might also slip in with news of enemy movements.

Troops practise wrestling to keep fit

DIPLOMACY

To avoid conflict whenever possible, ancient kings in the Middle East had a well-established diplomatic practice. Ambassadors, with special passports guaranteeing their safety, lived at foreign courts. Special messengers dashed between capital cities.

Presents and letters of goodwill were exchanged by the various rulers. The kings of Egypt, Babylon, the Mitanni and the Hittites called each other 'Brother'. Rulers of less powerful states addressed these monarchs as 'Father' or 'My Lord'.

'At the feet of the king, my Lord, my sun god, seven times seven times I fall. Let the king know that ever since his archers returned to Egypt Labíayu [a rival] has carried out attacks against me.'

Letter from the Prince of Megiddo to the Egyptian king

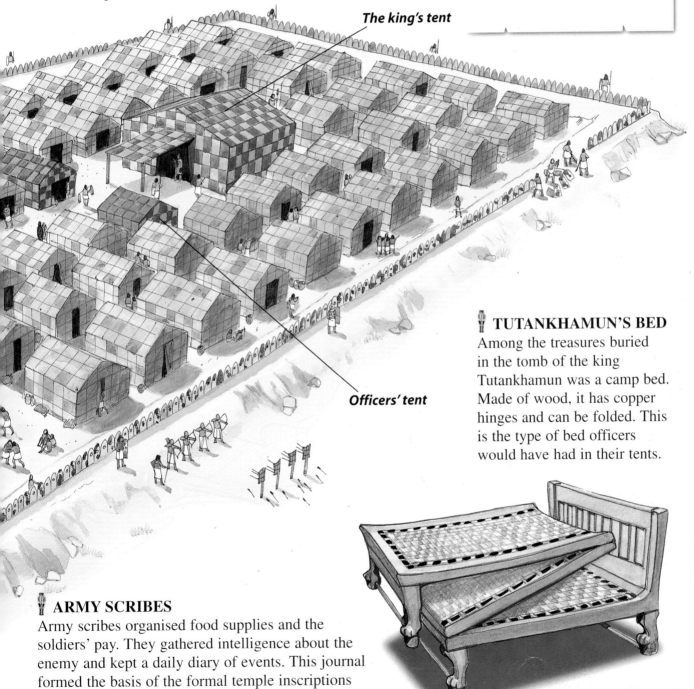

The king's tent

Officers' tent

TUTANKHAMUN'S BED

Among the treasures buried in the tomb of the king Tutankhamun was a camp bed. Made of wood, it has copper hinges and can be folded. This is the type of bed officers would have had in their tents.

ARMY SCRIBES

Army scribes organised food supplies and the soldiers' pay. They gathered intelligence about the enemy and kept a daily diary of events. This journal formed the basis of the formal temple inscriptions that described the king's great victories.

Tutankhamun's folding bed

23

GUARDING THE EMPIRE

Ramesses II led 20,000 troops on the Kadesh campaign in 1220BC, but this was not the entire Egyptian army. Garrisons were stationed in the great frontier fortresses and more divisions in permanent bases near major cities. Men rotated between campaigns, garrisons and bases.

Those in the bases lived in barracks, ten to a hut, but often had their families living nearby. A troop commander was in charge of an individual fort, garrison commanders were in charge of several forts and overseers of fortresses were responsible for all the forts on a particular frontier.

TRADE

Some trading expeditions required military protection. Incense was vital for the worship of the gods and the service of the dead, but it came from the far-off land of Punt. The journey involved crossing the Eastern Desert, then sailing down the Red Sea to bring back the precious incense and incense bushes. Soldiers were always needed to guard against attacks by hostile tribesmen and thieves who would try to steal the incense.

A successful expedition returns from Punt, a land far to the south of Egypt

GUARD DUTY

Some professional soldiers, supported by companies of conscripts, were sent on mining and quarrying expeditions. Mines – especially gold mines – and the caravans going to and from them had to be guarded. Managers of mines and quarries used criminals and prisoners of war to do the hard work. They had to be supervised and guarded to stop them escaping.

'Fortresses stand open – the walls and the battlements sleep peacefully – the police are stretched out asleep. The desert frontier guards are among the meadows where they like to be.'

King Ramesses III congratulates himself on establishing peace and security

24

Border guards outside a fortress

A garrison scribe at work

CHECKING THE FRONTIERS

Bedouin tribespeople from the Sinai region regularly came to Egypt seeking permission to enter the Delta and pasture their flocks on the rich vegetation. Entry was usually granted, but the border guards counted how many came in and made sure they all left later!

FOR THE RECORD

It was the duty of some of the scribes attached to garrisons to send the vizier (the king's chief minister) detailed written accounts of everything that happened in the garrison and along the frontiers.

An Egyptian repels a Peleset raider

TROUBLESHOOTERS

Troops and medjay (police) stationed in cities were there to defend them, but also to prevent any civil disturbances, to guard cemeteries and to catch criminals.

The Bedouin of the Sahara and the Eastern Desert were always ready to raid Egypt if they had the chance and in the time of the New Kingdom the Sea Peoples raided Egypt's northern coasts.

SEA BATTLES

Egypt had a strong navy and several naval dockyards. The one at Memphis was called 'Good Departure'. Egyptian soldiers were regularly transported by ship. Troops taken by sea to northern Canaan or by river to the southern frontier of Kush arrived fresher than if they had had a long, tiring march.

Egyptians fought many naval battles, including the great victory over the Sea Peoples in 1180BC. However, the sea battle that is best remembered is Actium (31BC). Losing it cost Queen Cleopatra VII her life and Egypt its independence.

SAILORS AND MARINES

On board ships sailors did the rowing and tended the sails. They wore leather kilts so their bottoms were not rubbed sore when they were rowing. A ship was commanded by a captain, assisted by a navigator. Ships were formed into squadrons under the 'Chief of Ships' – the admiral.

Quite separate from the sailors were the marines, who did the actual fighting. Large ships had up to 200 marines, led by a standard-bearer.

FIGHTING SHIPS

Ships were made of wooden planks, pegged and lashed together so they could easily be dismantled, carried over land or around a cataract, then quickly reassembled. Ships were propelled by oars and sails and guided by great steering oars. They were given names such as *Star of Memphis* and *The Ruler is Strong*. The king commanded naval expeditions and battles. His flagship was known as the *Falcon Ship*, after the god Horus.

NAVAL WARFARE

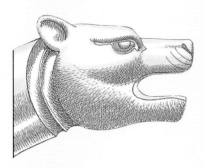

LIONS' HEADS
The bronze lions' heads fitted to the prows (bows) of Ramesses III's warships were not for decoration. They rammed, holed and sank enemy ships.

THE SEA PEOPLES
The Sea Peoples came from Mycenaean Greece and its colonies along the coast of Turkey and the Aegean Islands. Originally pirates and raiders, some eventually migrated south, first destroying the Hittite Empire and then threatening Egypt.

The Sea Peoples invade Egypt during the reign of Ramesses III, c.1180 BC

LOOKOUTS?
A famous tomb painting shows a ship transporting Nubian mercenaries. Were they lookouts? They certainly would have had a good view across the flat countryside through which they were travelling.

⍾ VICTORY
In c.1180BC, driven by failed harvests and the breakdown of law and order, thousands of Sea Peoples set out to find new homes. That meant taking land from someone else. Ramesses III stopped them in two great battles, one on land, one at sea. Egypt was fighting for its existence and all the reserves and conscripts were called up.

'Crocodiles are waiting, even while the boat is afloat! The sailor is worn out, the oar in his hand, the lash on his back and his belly is empty, but the scribe sits in the cabin.'

A teacher tries to persuade a pupil not to become a sailor

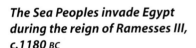

REWARDS FOR VALOUR

Some Egyptians joined the armed forces from a sense of duty to their king and country. Others wanted adventure, glory, a chance to make a fortune or a profession that could lead to promotion and advancement at court.

The New Kingdom army offered all these things – in varying degrees – to all ranks. Soldiers who took part in successful campaigns became heroes and, for the first time, young nobles could have a career outside the civil service or the priesthood. For ordinary men, the army offered the best way to become wealthy.

A soldier collects his rewards, including a Nubian slave girl

NEW LANDOWNERS
Soldiers who distinguished themselves in battle were given land to farm when they retired. This was a great incentive because many peasants did not own any land.

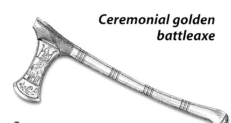

Ceremonial golden battleaxe

GOLD REWARDS
Soldiers could acquire valuables, such as the axe shown above. The Queen Mother Ahhotep, fighting on behalf of her son, was awarded three golden flies – Egypt's highest award for bravery.

Queen Ahhotep's golden flies

TREASURE AND SLAVES
Besides land, gold and medals, soldiers had a chance to win a fortune. When a city was captured, all the soldiers got a share of any treasure. In addition, they were given at least some of the male and female prisoners of war as slaves to keep or sell.

A young prince being handed over to a tutor

'I have grown old; I have reached old age. Favoured as before and loved by my Lord, I rest in the tomb that I myself made.'

The great soldier Ahmose, son of Ebana, celebrates his achievements in his tomb autobiography

Mummy of an Egyptian soldier

TRAINING A PRINCE

All princes were trained to be kings, for no one knew which one would live long enough to succeed his father as king.

A man, even one of humble origins, if he had had a highly successful army career could be honoured by being appointed the tutor of a young prince.

WINNING FAVOUR

At court it was difficult to get close to the king who was always surrounded by priests and courtiers. On campaign, however, even an ordinary soldier could attract his attention through bravery or a clever suggestion.

Kings tended to trust men who had served them well in war and, when peace came, often gave them important positions in the government and at court.

AFTERLIFE

Group of model soldiers

EQUIPMENT

A successful soldier who had been well rewarded for his services would be able to afford a tomb and proper burial equipment. This would include a *Book of the Dead* to guide him, model servants, a fine coffin and all his personal possessions.

THE KING'S FRIEND

Maiherpri was a great Nubian warrior and close friend of King Amenhotep II. He was granted the extraordinary honour of being buried in the Valley of the Kings, close to the king's own tomb.

GLOSSARY

Bedouin
Nomadic tribesmen who lived in the Eastern and Western Deserts.

Book of the Dead
Prayers and spells to help a dead person make the journey to the next world.

Bronze
Metal made from copper and tin.

Canaanites
People who lived in the land of Canaan – the modern countries of Israel, Jordan and Lebanon.

Cataract
Waterfall in a river. The Nile has six cataracts.

Cleopatra VII
Last of the Ptolemaic dynasty to rule Egypt. A good ruler, she was defeated when she backed Antony, the losing general in Rome's civil wars.

Conscript
Someone forced to join the armed forces.

Cuirass
Armour covering the upper part of the body.

Dynasty
A line of hereditary rulers.

Empire
Group of once independent states, ruled by a single person.

Hittites
People from the central area of what is now Turkey. They ruled an empire in the Middle East, and for many years were Egypt's rivals.

Horus
The special god of the Egyptian kings. He appeared as a hawk.

Hyksos
Invaders from Canaan, who conquered much of Egypt during the Second Intermediate Period (c.1790 – 1550BC).

Kush
The land between the Third and Fourth Cataracts of the Nile. Its capital was at Kerma. The Egyptians conquered it around 1500BC.

Labour tax
Money was not invented until the Late Period (664 – 332BC). Before that taxes were paid to the king in work and goods (things you grew or made). The work included digging irrigation canals, working in quarries or serving in the army.

Medjay
Soldiers who were originally Nubian mercenaries, but later became a police force in Egypt.

Memphis
City on the west bank of the Nile, just south of modern Cairo. It was founded by Menes as the capital of united Egypt.

Mercenary
Professional soldier employed by a foreign state.

Middle Kingdom
Period in Egypt's history from about 2040 to 1790BC.

Mitanni
The people who, for a time, ruled the land around the upper reaches of the River Euphrates in modern Iraq. They were wiped out by the Hittites.

Mycenae
Greek city where a fine civilization flourished from c.1900 to c.1100BC.

New Kingdom
Period in Egyptian history from about 1550 to 1080BC.

Nile

Egypt has very little rainfall, so the River Nile is Egypt's main source of water. Each year, before the building of modern dams, it flooded the flat land, bringing water and rich black mud to the fields.

Nile Delta

Lower (Northern) Egypt. It is the area downstream from the modern city of Cairo, where the Nile divides into several channels and flows to the Mediterranean Sea.

Nomarch

District governor during the Old and Middle Kingdoms. Egypt had 42 nomes (administrative districts), each ruled by a nomarch.

Nubia

The land between the Nile's First and Third Cataracts.

Old Kingdom

Period in Egypt's history from about 2700 to 2100BC.

Peleset

A group of the Sea Peoples. After their defeat by Ramesses III they settled in the land named after them: Palestine. In the Old Testament of the Bible they are the Philistines.

Punt

The source of incense for the ancient world. It is now thought to be Somalia.

Ramesses II

Famous for the Battle of Kadesh, which he claimed to have won single-handed. He was also a great builder of temples.

Ramesses III

Descended from Ramesses II, Ramesses III saved Egypt from invasion by the Sea Peoples.

Re

The ancient Egyptians' chief sun god.

Scout

Person sent out from an army to discover where the enemy is.

Scribe

Someone who can read and write and makes a living by doing so.

Sea Peoples

Peoples thought to be from Mycenaean Greece, its colonies on the west coast of Turkey and the Aegean Islands. Driven from their homelands by famine and unrest, they destroyed many cities and wiped out the Hittite Empire.

Eventually they were defeated by Ramesses III.

Senusret III

One of Egypt's greatest warrior kings, he ruled c.1870BC. He strengthened the fortresses around the Second Cataract and fought the Kushites.

Sherden

One of the Sea Peoples. When some were captured by the Egyptians, they became part of the royal bodyguard.

Stela

An inscribed stone commemoration slab.

Thebes

City on the East Bank of the Nile in Upper Egypt, it is now called Luxor.

Tribute

Taxes paid by defeated peoples to their conquerors.

Tuthmosis III

Ruler during the New Kingdom and perhaps the greatest of all Egypt's warrior kings.

Valley of the Kings

Situated on the West Bank of the Nile, opposite Thebes. Most of the New Kingdom kings were buried there.

INDEX

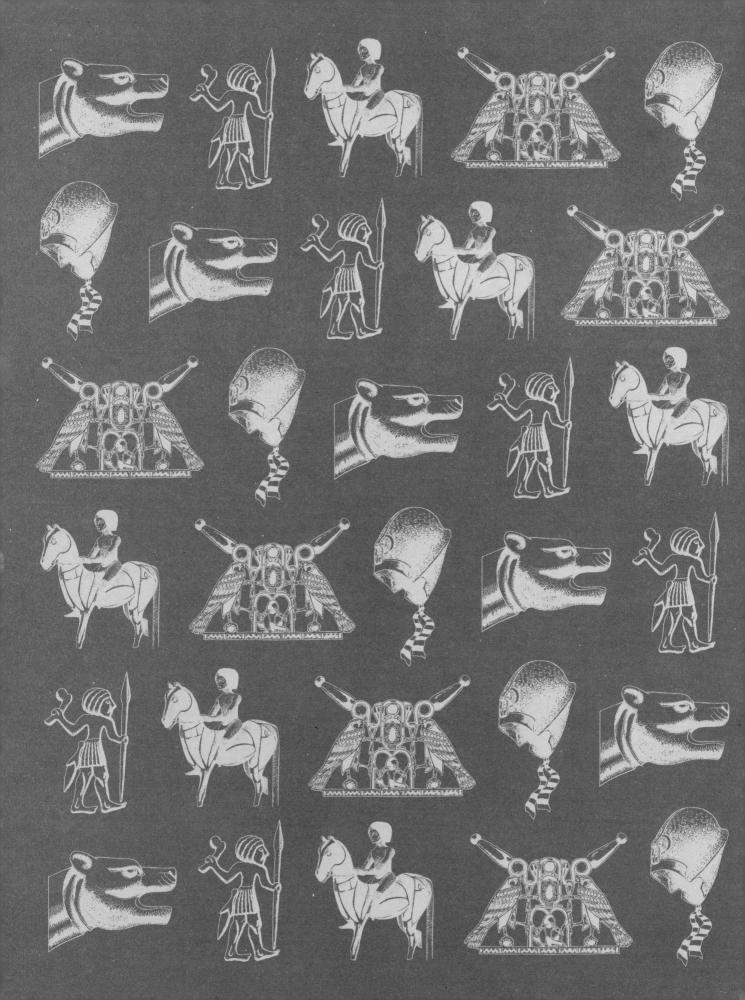